Charles H. Jones

A Digest of the Acts of Assembly and Ordinances of Councils

Relating to Fairmount Park

Charles H. Jones

A Digest of the Acts of Assembly and Ordinances of Councils Relating to Fairmount Park

ISBN/EAN: 9783337289041

Printed in Europe, USA, Canada, Australia, Japan

Cover: Foto ©Suzi / pixelio.de

More available books at **www.hansebooks.com**

A DIGEST

OF THE

Acts of Assembly and Ordinances of Councils

RELATING TO

FAIRMOUNT PARK.

BY

CHARLES HENRY JONES,

SOLICITOR TO THE PARK COMMISSIONERS.

PHILADELPHIA:

KING & BAIRD, PRINTERS, 607 SANSOM STREET.

1872.

At a meeting of the Commissioners of Fairmount Park, held June 15th, 1872, the following resolution was adopted:

Resolved, That the Park Solicitor be requested to prepare a digest of the acts of Assembly and ordinances of the City Councils relating to Fairmount Park.

(2)

INDEX.

CARE.

And management. Commissioners to have, of the Park on
both banks of the Schuylkill......................23, 35

CHIEF ENGINEER AND SURVEYOR.

To be one of the Park Commissioners......................20

CHIEF ENGINEER OF THE WATER WORKS.

To be one of the Park Commissioners......................20

CITY OF PHILADELPHIA.

See Philadelphia, City of.

CITY PROPERTY.

Commissioner of, to be one of the Park Commissioners......20

COMMISSIONERS OF FAIRMOUNT PARK.

How appointed..20
To organize annually...................................20
To elect president and secretary annually..............20
Vacancies in, how filled...............................21
To receive no compensation for their services..........21
To petition for jury...................................21
May negotiate and agree with owners of ground as to the
  price thereof... ....21, 60
To make report of their agreements with owners of ground
  to Court of Quarter Sessions.........................21
Shall adopt a plan for the improvement and maintenance of
  the Park and proceed with the same.................23, 35
All moneys expended to be under supervision of.........23
To have the care and management of the Park on both
  banks of the Schuylkill.............................23, 35
Authorized to lay out Roberts' Hollow drive...........27, 57
To make and file survey of Roberts' Hollow drive.......28
To appropriate the shores of the Wissahickon Creek.....28
To make and file survey of grounds upon Wissahickon
  creek..28
To have all the power and control over ground appropri-
  ated by act of 1868, given them by act of 1867.....29, 47, 60
May vacate any street or road within the Park, except
  Girard avenue..29
May open roads, avenues and streets in the Park for pub-
  lic use..29
To have jurisdiction over footway next the Park in all
  boundary avenues.....................................30

CONTRACTS.

COUNCILS.

DAMAGES.

DEBTS.

GROUND.

INDEX.

LIENS AND INCUMBRANCES.

Land taken for public use is divested of all.........note (*a*) 28
The court will not award the damages assessed where
there are liens and incumbrances, without making an
equitable distribution of the fund...............note (*a*) 28
Must be taken from the fund before the report of the jury
is confirmed.................................note (*a*) 28

LOANS.

City to raise money by loans for all grounds, the laying out
and construction, permanent care and improvement
thereof and for all culverts............................32
City to provide for payment of interest on loans and sinking fund for their redemption.......................32

MAINTENANCE.

Commissioners to adopt plan for the maintenance of the
Park and proceed with the same..................23, 35

MANAGEMENT.

Commissioners to have management of the Park on both
banks of the Schuylkill.........................23, 35

MANUFACTORIES.

Commissioners may exclude manufactories from the Park....53

MAYOR.

Of the city to be one of the Park Commissioners 20
Park police to be subject to orders of Mayor in any emergency..41

MONEYS.

All moneys expended to be under supervision of Commis-
sioners...23
All moneys paid into city treasury by Commissioners to be
exclusively appropriated for Park purposes.............41
All moneys raised for purchase of grounds, etc., to be kept
separately by city treasurer...........................44
Councils shall provide such moneys for Hunting Park as
Commissioners may require..........................68

NOTICE.

Commissioners to give notice of taking possession of ground...21
Commissioners may take possession of property after sixty
days' notice..44

PENALTY.

PHILADELPHIA, CITY OF.

POSSESSION.

FAIRMOUNT PARK.

ACTS OF ASSEMBLY

Act of March 26, 1867. P. L. 547.

AN ACT

Appropriating ground for public purposes, in the City of Philadelphia.

SECTION 1. *Be it enacted by the Senate and House of Representatives of the Commonwealth of Pennsylvania in General Assembly met, and it is hereby enacted by the authority of same.* That the title to, and ownership of, the area of ground which is bounded as follows ;(a) Beginning at a point on the river Schuylkill, at the intersection of the north line of Bridge street and low water mark in said river; thence along said north line of Bridge street, to Bridgewater street; thence along the easterly side of Bridgewater street, to north line of Haverford street, as now used; thence along the northeast line of said Haverford street to the Pennsylvania railroad; thence along said Pennsylvania railroad, to the Junction railroad; thence along the said Junction railroad, its several courses and distances, to a point where it intersects

Boundaries of Fairmount Park described.

(a) Boundary of the Park modified by Act of April 14, 1868, Sec. 1, post, page 25. See also, Sec. 4 of said Act, post, page 29.

(19)

Girard avenue; thence westwardly, along the north line
of Girard avenue, to Forty-first street; thence northward,
along Forty-first street, to Lansdowne avenue; thence
along said Lansdowne avenue, westwardly, to Belmont
avenue; thence along said Belmont avenue, northwardly,
to Montgomery avenue; thence eastward, along said Montgomery avenue, in a direct line, to the water line of Fairmount dam; thence down the river Schuylkill, along the
low water line thereof, to the place of beginning, excepting therefrom and thereout, that part of which the Schuylkill Navigation, the Pennsylvania Central, the Junction
and the Connecting Railroad Companies, are respectively
seized, for the execution of their franchises,(a) shall be
vested in the City of Philadelphia, to be laid out and
maintained forever, as an open public place and park, for
the health and enjoyment of the people of said city, and
the preservation of the purity of the water supply of the
City of Philadelphia.

Franchises of Schuylkill Navigation Company, Pennsylva-nia, Junction and Connec-ting Railroad Companies, excepted.

Commis-sioners

SECT. 2. That the Mayor, the Presidents of the Select
and Common Councils, Commissioner of City Property,
the Chief Engineer and Surveyor, and the Chief Engineer
of the Water Works of said city, together with ten citizens of said city, who shall be appointed for five years,
five of them by the District Court, and five of them by
the Court of Common Pleas of said city, be and the same
are hereby constituted Commissioners of said Park; they
shall organize annually on the first Monday of June, by
the election of a president and secretary,(b) but they shall

To organize annually.

(a) See also, Sec. 3 Act of April 14, 1868, post, page 28.

(b) So much of the section as requires that the Secretary shall be
chosen from the Commissioners, repealed by Act of April 14, 1868,
Sec. 12, post, page 33.

receive no compensation for their services as Commis- To receive no compensation.
sioners: *Provided*, That whenever a vacancy shall occur
in that part of the said Commissioners appointed by the Vacancies, how filled.
courts, the court from which the appointment was made
shall fill the vacancy.

SECT. 3. That the owners of the said ground,(*a*) by the Owners of ground to be
first section of this act appropriated for public purposes, paid for the same by the
shall be paid(*b*) for the same by the City of Philadelphia, city.
according to the value(*c*) which shall be ascertained by a Value, how ascertained.
jury of twelve(*d*)disinterested freeholders, to be appointed(*e*)
by the Court of Quarter Sessions of said city, upon the Commissioners to petition for
petition of said Commissioners; and if the said Commis- jury.
sioners shall delay petitioning as aforesaid for the period
of sixty days after notice given of their taking possession Owners may petition for
of said ground, then said jury shall be appointed upon jury if Commissioners
the petition of any person whose property shall be so delay for sixty days.
taken: *Provided, however,* That in any case the said Commissioners may negotiate and agree with the owners of Commissioners may ne-
any part of said ground as to the price thereof, and said gotiate and agree with
price shall be reported to the said Court of Quarter Ses- owners of ground.

(*a*) A tenant for years is such an owner : 4 Wh. 90 ; 8 II. 91 ; 10 II.
29 ; 1 C. 229 ; 16 P. F. Smith, 425. A ground landlord is not such an
owner : 6 C. 362. See 28 Leg. Int. 356. The purchaser of an estate
cannot claim damages for an injury done to it before his purchase.
Such claim remains in the hands of the vendor : 10 II. 32.

(*b*) Either under the Act of April 14, 1868, or by a common law
action of debt, the land owner may recover the damages assessed or
agreed on immediately upon confirmation of the report relating to
damages : 18 P. F. Smith, 49.

(*c*) The basis of compensation is not to be measured solely by the
value of the land taken. The advantages likely to accrue, enter
largely into the estimate : 4 II. 192 ; 11 Wright, 435 ; 29 Leg. Int. 220.

(*d*) Reduced to six by Sec. 10 of the Act of April 14, 1868, post,
page 31.

(*e*) See Act of January 27, 1870, Sec. 3, post, page 49.

sions, and if confirmed and approved by said court, shall
be conclusive upon said city: *And provided further*, That

Jury to assess advantages upon land adjoining and in the vicinity of the Park. And proceed according to the road laws.

whenever it shall be necessary to have recourse to a
jury to assess the damages for any property to be taken
as aforesaid [the said jury shall estimate the advantage
to property adjoining or in the vicinity(*a*) and](*b*)
said jury(*c*) shall proceed and their award shall be reviewed and enforced in the same manner as provided by
law in the opening of roads in the City of Philadelphia.(*d*)

Commissioners to adopt plan for improvement, &c. of Park.

SECT. 4. That the Commissioners of the said Park, after
they shall have secured possession of the ground, shall

(*a*) The term vicinity does not denote any particular, definite distance from the Park : 6 H. 26. Such assessments are constitutional :
3 W. 296 ; 7 Barr 175 ; 6 H. 26 ; 3 Philadelphia, 265 ; 11 C. 231 ; 22 Leg.
Int. (1865) 365 ; 4 N. Y. (4 Comst.) 419 ; 8 Wendell, 85 ; Ibid. 101 ;
3 Paige, 45 ; 7 Hill, 9 ; 5 Ohio State Reports, 636 ; 19 Ohio, 418 ; 26
Ill. 351 ; 30 Mo. 537.

(*b*) Repealed by Act of June 15, 1871, post, page 54.

(*c*) See Act of January 27, 1870, Sec. 3, post, page 49.

(*d*) See Act of April 14, 1868, Sec. 10, post, page 31. See also,
18 P. F. Smith, 47. When the Court of Quarter Sessions have appointed a full set of jurors, one or more of the number may be
stricken off and others substituted, and it is not necessary to give
notice that it will be done : 3 C. 69. The jury must be sworn before
they enter upon their duties : 2 P. R. 207. And it must be stated in
the report : 3 S. & R. 210. See 4 Wh. 514. Any of the jurors are
competent to administer an oath to one of their number : 2 C. 222.
The report of the jury must be accompanied by a draft : 3 Binney, 3 ;
10 S. & R. 120. Five of the six jurors appointed must view the property : 6 H. 220 ; 3 C. 69. All the jurors must deliberate, but a
majority may decide : 5 C. 20. It is no objection to the report of
viewers appointed to assess damages, that they conversed with the
owners of property adjoining, in the absence of the parties interested.
An inquest of this sort is restrained to no peculiar species of evidence,
and may resort to any source of information which the members of it
may think proper, even the evidence of their senses : 4 R. 192. The
jury are to judge for themselves on view of the premises, and not by
the opinions of witnesses : 2 Wh. 277. The jury are to consider the
matter just as if they were called on to value the injury at the moment
when compensation could first be demanded : 11 Wr. 434.

adopt a plan for the improvement and maintenance thereof, and shall have power to proceed with the same, and all moneys expended shall be under their supervision, but no contracts shall be made for said improvement unless an appropriation therefor shall have been first made by the Councils of said city.(a)

Expenditure of all moneys to be under their supervision.

No contract to be made before appropriation is made.

SECT. 5. That as soon as the said Commissioners shall have fully organized, they shall have the care and management of Fairmount Park, on both banks of the river Schuylkill, and all plans and expenditures for the improvement and maintenance of the same shall be under their control, subject to such appropriations(a) as Councils may from time to time make as aforesaid.(b)

Commissioners to have care of Fairmount Park and all plans to be under their control.

[SECT. 6. That the Commissioners of said Park are hereby further empowered, whenever the Councils of the City of Philadelphia shall so declare by ordinance, to take such other land as may be deemed proper by said Councils for the extension of said Fairmount Park, between the Spring Garden Water Works and the Columbia Bridge and between the Reading Railroad and the river Schuylkill, according to the value which shall be ascertained by a jury of twelve disinterested freeholders, to be appointed by the Court of Quarter Sessions of said city upon the petition of said commissioners ; and if the said commissioners shall delay petitioning as aforesaid for a period of sixty days after notice given of their taking possession of said ground, then said jury shall be ap-

Commissioners authorized (when Councils shall so declare) to take other land for extension of Park.

(a) See Act of April 14, 1868, Sec. 11, post, page 32, and Sec. 19, post, page 35.
(b) See preceding section.

Proviso.

pointed upon the petition of any person whose property shall be so taken. *Provided, however,* That in any case the said Commissioners may negotiate directly and agree with the owners of any part of said ground as to the price thereof, and said price shall be reported to the said Court of Quarter Sessions, and if confirmed or approved by said court, shall be conclusive upon said city: *And*

Proviso.

provided further, That whenever it shall be necessary to have recourse to a jury to assess the damages for any property to be taken as aforesaid, the said jury shall estimate the advantage to property adjoining or in the vicinity, and said jury shall proceed, and their award shall be reviewed and enforced in the same manner as provided by law in the opening of roads in the City of Philadelphia.](*a*)

(*a*) The provisions of this section are supplied by subsequent legislation. The land referred to therein is included within the Park boundaries by the Act of April 14, 1868, Sec. 1, post, page 25, and the other provisions are also supplied by the Act of April 14, 1868, Sec. 5, post, page 29, and Sec. 26, post page 41, and the Act of March 26, 1867, Sec. 3, ante, page 21.

Act of April 14, 1868. P. L. 1083.

A SUPPLEMENT

To an act, entitled "An act appropriating ground for public purposes, in the City of Philadelphia," approved the twenty-sixth day of March, Anno Domini one thousand eight hundred and sixty-seven.

SECTION 1. *Be it enacted by the Senate and House of Representatives of the Commonwealth of Pennsylvania in General Assembly met, and it is hereby enacted by the authority of the same,* That the boundaries of the Fairmount Park in the City of Philadelphia shall be the following, to wit: Beginning at a point in the northeasterly line of property owned and occupied by the Reading Railroad Company, near the City bridge over the river Schuylkill at the Falls, where said northeasterly line [is intersected by the line dividing property of H. Duhring from that of F. Stoever and T. Johnson ; extending](a) from thence in a southwesterly direction upon said dividing line and its prolongation to the middle of the Ford road ; from thence by a line passing through the southeast corner of Forty-ninth and Lebanon streets to George's run ; thence along the several courses of said run to a point fourteen hundred and eighty-seven and a half feet from the middle of the Pennsylvania Railroad, measured at right angles thereto ; thence by a straight line through the northeast corner of Forty-third and Hancock streets to the northerly side of Girard avenue near Fortieth street; thence by the said northerly side of Girard avenue to the easterly side of the

Boundaries of Fairmount Park defined.

(a) Amended by Act of April 21, 1869, Sec. 8, post, page 46.

Junction railroad as now used; thence by the said easterly side of the Junction railroad and the Pennsylvania
railroad to the north side of Haverford street; thence by
the northerly side of said Haverford street to the westerly
side of Bridgewater street; thence by said Bridgewater
street to the north line of Bridge street; thence by said
Bridge street to the west abutment of the Suspension
bridge; thence by the northwesterly side of the Suspension bridge and Callowhill street to the angle in said
street, on the southwesterly side of Fairmount basin;
thence by the northerly side of Callowhill and Biddle
streets to the westerly side of Twenty-fifth street; thence
by the said Twenty-fifth street to the southwesterly side
of Pennsylvania avenue; thence by the southwesterly
side of Pennsylvania avenue to the west side of Thirty-
third street; thence along the westerly side of Thirty-
third street to the southwesterly line of Ridge avenue;
thence along said Ridge avenue to the southwesterly line
of South Laurel Hill Cemetery (north of Huntingdon
street); thence by and along said property line to such a
distance from the shore line of the river Schuylkill as
will permit the location of a carriage road one hundred
feet wide upon its margin; thence along said river shore
and its several courses as may be most practicable, at the
same distance as above specified (provided said distance
shall not exceed one hundred and fifty feet), to a point
opposite the intersection of the Ridge turnpike and
School lane; thence northwardly to a point on the southwesterly side of said turnpike road opposite to the southeasterly side of said School lane; thence by the southwesterly side of the Ridge turnpike road and its several
courses to the southeasterly side of the Wissahickon

creek; thence by the several courses of the said south-easterly side of Wissahickon creek to the Schuylkill river; thence across the water course of said river to the northeasterly line of the Reading Railroad Company's property as now occupied and in use, at the City boundary line; thence along said northeasterly line, as now occupied and used by said railroad company, to the place of beginning ;(a) excepting, nevertheless, thereout the several water works and their appurtenances, which are included within these boundaries, and such uses of the premises immediately adjacent to the same, and such other portions of the ground as are described in the plan, as the City of Philadelphia may from time to time require for the purposes of its water department.(b)

Water works excepted.

SECT. 2. That there shall be laid out and constructed a road of easy and practicable grades extending from the intersection of the northerly line of the Park by Belmont avenue on the westerly side of the river Schuylkill to the head of Roberts' Hollow, and thence along said hollow and the river Schuylkill to the foot of City avenue, laid out with the ground contiguous thereto for ornamentation, of such width and so constructed as the Commissioners of Fairmount Park, appointed under authority of the act of the General Assembly of the Commonwealth,(c) may determine. And such road and its contiguous ground are hereby declared to be a part of the aforesaid Park; and said Park Commissioners are hereby authorized and re-

Roberts' Hollow drive authorized.

And declared part of the Park.

(a) See Act of April 21, 1869, Sec. 2, post, page 43, and Sec. 5, post, page 45.

(b) See, for further exceptions, Act of April 14, 1868, Sec. 3, post, page 28. See also Act of March 15, 1871, Sec. 1, post, page 53, and Act of March 26, 1867, Sec. 1, ante, page 20.

(c) See Act of March 26, 1867, Section 2, ante, page 20.

Commissioners to make and file survey thereof.

Wissahickon creek and its shores appropriated

quired to ascertain, by a proper survey, the limits thereof, which survey they shall file in the Survey Department of the City of Philadelphia. And it shall also be the duty of said Park Commissioners to appropriate the shores of the Wissahickon creek on both sides of the same from its mouth to the Paul's Mill road, and of such width as may embrace the road now passing along the same; and may also protect the purity of the water of said creek, and by passing along the crest of the heights which are on either side of said creek, may preserve the beauty of its scenery.

Commissioners to make and file survey thereof.

Declared part of the Park.

The said Park Commissioners are hereby authorized and required to cause a proper survey to be made of said grounds upon the Wissahickon, and to file said survey in the Survey Department of the City of Philadelphia, and the grounds and creek hereby appropriated are declared to be a part of Fairmount Park.

Title to Park vested in the City.

Excepting franchises of Schuylkill Navigation, Philadelphia and Reading, Junction and Connecting Railroad Companies.

SECT. 3. That the title to and ownership of the ground within said boundaries shall be vested(a) in the City of Philadelphia, excepting therefrom so much as shall be required by the Schuylkill Navigation Company, the Philadelphia and Reading, the Junction and Connecting Rail-

(a) Land taken for public use is divested of all liens and incumbrances : 24 Leg. Int. 61 ; 27 Leg. Int. 61. But the court will not award the damages assessed, without inquiring whether there are any incumbrances, and if there are, an equitable distribution of the fund will be made : 1 Ashmead, 276 ; 5 Wr. 470. The power of the court must be exercised before the report of the jury is confirmed : 4 P. L. J. 468. Where damages have been assessed or agreed on for land taken for Fairmount Park, the land vested in the City of Philadelphia, and if the landowner continues in possession, it is at sufferance, and he can be turned out at any time : 18 P. F. Smith, 49. See also Act of April 21, 1859, Sec. 4, post, page 44, and Act of April 14, 1868, Sec. 9, post page 31.

road Companies for the execution of their franchises as now provided by law.(a)

SECT. 4. So much of the ground as was embraced in the act to which this is a supplement, approved the twenty-sixth day of March, one thousand eight hundred and sixty-seven, and is not included in the above boundaries,(b) is hereby released from all claim of title by the said city, with the same effect as if it had never been included.(c)

Claim of City to portion of ground embraced in Act of 1867 released.

SECT. 5. That all the grounds taken within the bound-aries of the Fairmount Park by the first section of this act, shall be subject to all the powers and control given by the act to which this is a supplement to the City of Philadelphia and the Park Commissioners designated by or appointed under said act ;(d) and the owners of all ground taken for the Park, and others interested therein, shall be compensated as in said act is directed and provided.(e)

All Park grounds to be subject to all powers conferred by the Act of 1867.

And owners of ground shall be compensated as therein provided.

SECT. 6. The said Commissioners shall have power and authority, from time to time, to vacate any street or road within the boundaries of the Park (excepting Girard avenue), and to open for public use such other roads, avenues and streets therein as they may deem necessary.

Commissioners may vacate streets, except Girard avenue, and open other roads, &c.

(a) See Act of April 14, 1868, Sec. 1, ante, page 27, for further exception.

(b) See ante, Sec. 1, page 25, and Sec. 2, page 27.

(c) See Act of March 26, 1867, Sec. 1, ante, page 19. This release applies only to the triangular piece of ground bounded by Girard avenue, Forty-first street and Elm avenue.

(d) Act of March 26, 1867, ante, page 19. See also Act of April 21, 1869, Sec. 8, post, page 46.

(e) See Act of April 14, 1868, Sec. 26, post, page 41. See also Act of March 26, 1867, Section 3, ante, page 21.

Councils shall cause alterations of the plan of survey in the 24th, 20th and 28th Wards.

SECT. 7. The Councils of the City of Philadelphia shall cause, under the supervision of the Department of Surveys, such alterations of the plan of survey of the Twenty-fourth Ward as lies between Fairmount Park as by this act established, the Pennsylvania railroad and the City avenue, and of the contiguous parts of the Twentieth(a)and Twenty-eighth Wards, as may become necessary or expedient by reason of the extension as aforesaid of the limits of the Fairmount Park, and cause the same to be established in manner as now provided by law for revising or laying out plans of survey in and for the City of Philadelphia; and

And lay out a boundary avenue around the Park.

shall lay out an avenue as one of the streets of the city, of the width of not less than one hundred feet, as a boundary of the Park on the southwest, west and northwest sides thereof, extending from Girard avenue to the river Schuylkill, at or near the Falls Bridge; and also upon the eastern side of the river from the intersection of Pennsylvania avenue and Thirty-third street, northward along the boundary of said Park to the river Schuylkill.

Jurisdiction of Commissioners shall extend over footway of boundary avenues next the Park. Width of footways.

SECT. 8. The jurisdiction of the Commissioners of the Park shall extend to the breadth of the footway next the Park, in all avenues or streets which shall bound upon the Park, and they shall direct the manner in which such footways shall be laid out, curbed, paved, planted and ornamented; which footways shall not be less than twenty feet in width on any avenue or street of the width of one hundred feet, and of like proportion upon any street or avenue of a greater or less width, unless otherwise directed by the Commissioners.

(a) A new ward has been created out of that part of the Twentieth Ward, contiguous to the Park since this act was passed, called the Twenty-ninth Ward.

SECT. 9. The said Park Commissioners or jury who shall assess the compensation to the owners for the ground taken, shall ascertain and make compensation for buildings,(a) as well as the ground taken; but all buildings and machinery and fixtures not required by the Park Commission, shall be removed by the owners thereof whenever payment of the compensation awarded them shall be made or tendered to them; and upon such payment or tender, the Park Commissioners shall forthwith take possession of the premises.(b) If any owner or lessee of ground taken cannot be found, notice of the taking and valuation of his land shall be given by advertisement in two daily papers, published in Philadelphia, six times, and in the Legal Intelligencer twice; and the amount awarded in such case to the owner or lessee, shall remain in the city treasury, until such owner shall produce the decree of the court having jurisdiction in the premises, ordering the said moneys to be paid to him or his legal representatives.

Compensation to be made for buildings as well as ground taken. Buildings, machinery and fixtures not required by Commissioners to be removed by owners, whenever payment of damages is tendered them. Proceedings where owner or lessee of ground taken cannot be found.

SECT. 10. The said Commissioners and jury may make partial or special reports, from time to time, to the court, as they may be ready to do so, and the court may act upon such reports separately;(c) and the powers of the jury shall continue, unless limited by the court, or they be required by the court to make report, until they shall have reported on all the cases on which they have been appointed, although a term or terms of the court shall have intervened; and jurors, not to exceed six in number,

Commissioners and jury may make partial reports. Powers of the jury to continue until they have reported on all their cases, unless otherwise ordered by the court.

(a) See Act of March 15, 1871, Sec. 1, post, page 53.
(b) See ante, page 28, note (a). See also Act of April 21, 1869. Sec. 4, post, page 44.
(c) See Act of January 27, 1870, Sec. 1, post, page 48. See also ante, page 22, note (d).

Six jurors may be appointed on one or more cases.

Valuation forthwith payable upon confirmation of the report.

City to raise money by loans for all grounds; the laying out and construction, permanent care and improvement thereof, and for all culverts.

Shall assess taxes for keeping the Park in repair. And provide for payment of interest, and loans.

Commissioners to appoint officers, agents, &c., and prescribe their duties and compensation.

may be appointed upon one or more cases, according to the order of the court made; and whenever any report of the said Commissioners or of the jury shall have been confirmed by the court, the valuation made shall be forthwith payable by the City of Philadelphia.(*a*)

SECT. 11. The City of Philadelphia shall be authorized and required to raise by loans, from time to time, such sums of money(*b*) as shall be necessary to make compensation for all grounds heretofore taken or to be taken for said Fairmount Park, and for the laying out and construction thereof for public use; for the permanent care and improvement thereof, and for all culverts and other means for preserving the Schuylkill water pure for the use of the citizens of said city, and shall annually assess taxes for keeping in repair and good order the said Park; and shall also provide for the payment of the interest on all said loans, and the usual sinking fund for the redemption thereof.

SECT. 12. The said Park Commissioners shall, from time to time, appoint such officers, agents and subordinates as they may deem necessary, for the purposes of this act and the act to which this is a supplement; (*c*) and they shall prescribe the duties and the compensation to

(*a*) The Legislature may direct the *time* for paying damages assessed for taking property for public use: 18 P. F. Smith 45. The price of land taken for Fairmount Park as agreed upon with the Commissioners bears interest from the day of the confirmation of their report by the court, not from the date of the agreement: Ibid. 48. As to interest on awards made after April 21, 1869, see Act of April 21, 1869, Sec 9, post, page 47.

(*b*) See Act of April 21, 1869, Sec. 3, post, page 44.

(*c*) See Act of April 14, 1868, Sec. 27, post, page 41, and also Act of January 27, 1870, Sec. 5, post, page 49.

be paid them; and so much of the second section(*a*) of the act to which this is a supplement, as requires that the Secretary shall be chosen from the Commissioners, be and the same is hereby repealed.

(marginal note: Repeal of provision of Act of 1867, relating to election of Secretary.)

SECT. 13. It shall be lawful for said Park Commissioners to acquire title to the whole of any tract of land, part of which shall fall within the boundaries mentioned in the first section of this act, and to take conveyance thereof in the name of the City of Philadelphia ; and such part thereof as shall lie beyond or [within](*b*) the said Park limits, again to sell and convey in absolute fee simple to any purchaser or purchasers thereof, by deeds to be signed by the Mayor, under the seal of the city, to be affixed by direction of Councils ; either for cash, or part cash and part to be secured by bond and mortgage to the city, paying all cash into the city treasury : *Provided*, That the proceeds of such sales shall be paid into the sinking fund for the redemption of the loan created under the provisions of this act: *Provided also*, That no Commissioner, nor any officer under the Park Commission, shall in any wise be directly or indirectly interested in any such sale of lands by the Commissioners as aforesaid ; and if any Commissioner or officer aforesaid shall act in violation of this proviso, he shall, if a Commissioner, be subject to expulsion; if an officer, to be discharged by a majority of votes of the Board of Park Commissioners, after an opportunity afforded of explanation and defence.

(marginal note: Commissioners may acquire the whole of a tract of land where part of it lies within the Park.)

(marginal note: And sell parts thereof lying outside the Park.)

(marginal note: Terms of sale.)

(marginal note: Proceeds of sales to be paid into the sinking fund.)

(marginal note: No commissioner or officer shall be interested in such sales under penalty of discharge.)

(*a*) Ante, page 20.
(*b*) Altered to "without" by Sec. 2, of the Act of January 27, 1870, post, page 48.

3

Commissioners to report annually to the Mayor.

SECT. 14. The said Board of Commissioners shall, annually hereafter, [in the month of December, make, to the Mayor of the City of Philadelphia,](a) a report of their proceedings, and a statement of their expenditures for the preceding year.

May lease houses, &c., within Park limits.

SECT. 15. The said Park Commissioners shall have exclusive power to lease from year to year, all houses and buildings within the Park limits, which may be let without prejudice to the interests and purposes of the Park,

To collect rents and pay them into City Treasury.

by leases to be signed by their President and Secretary, and to collect the rents and pay them into the city treasury.

Buildings erected on Park grounds by boat clubs, &c., relative to.

SECT. 16. All houses and buildings now built or to be built on any part of the Park grounds, by or for boat or skating clubs, or zoological or other purposes, shall be taken to have rights subordinate to the public purposes intended to be subserved by acquiring and laying out the Park, and shall be subject to the regulations of said Park Commissioners, under licenses which shall be approved by the Commission, and signed by the President and Secretary, and will subject them to their supervision and to removal, or surrender to the city, whensoever the said Commissioners may require.

Commissioners may accept devises, &c., of property

SECT. 17. The said Park Commissioners shall have power to accept, in the name and behalf of the City of Philadelphia, devises, bequests and donations of lands,

(a) Amended by Sec. 4, of the Act of January 27, 1870, to read "to the Councils of the City of Philadelphia during the month of January." See post, page 49.

moneys, objects of art and natural history, maps and books, or other things, upon such trusts as may be prescribed by the testator or donor: *Provided*, Such trusts be satisfactory to the Commission, and compatible with the purposes of said Park.

in trust for the purposes of the Park.

SECT. 18. None of the Park Commissioners, nor any person employed by them, shall have power to create any debt or obligation to bind said Board of Commissioners, except by the express authority of the said Commissioners at a meeting duly convened.

Debts to be created only by Commissioners at a regular meeting.

SECT. 19. The said Park Commissioners shall have the power to govern, manage, lay out, plant and ornament the said Fairmount Park, and to maintain the same in good order and repair;(*a*) and to construct all proper bridges, buildings, railways,(*b*) and other improvements therein, and to repress all disorders therein under the provisions hereinafter contained.(*c*)

Commissioners to have power to manage and lay out the Park.

SECT. 20. That the said Park Commissioners shall have authority to license the laying down, and the use for a term of years, from time to time, of such passenger railways as they may think will comport with the use and enjoyment of the said Park by the public, upon such terms as said Commissioners may agree; all emoluments from which shall be paid into the city treasury.(*b*)

Commissioners may license passenger railways in the Park.

SECT. 21. The said Park shall be under the following

Rules and Regulations.

(*a*) See also Act of March 26, 1867, Sec. 4, ante, page 22, and Sec. 5, ante, page 23.
(*b*) See Act of March 16, 1870, Sec. 1, post, page 51.
(*c*) See post, Sec. 21.

rules and regulations, and such others as the Park Commissioners may from time to time ordain :(*a*)

(*a*) The following additional rules and regulations have been ordained by the Park Commissioners :

I. No person shall throw any dead animal or offensive matter or substance of any kind, into the river Schuylkill, within the boundaries of Fairmount Park.

II. No person shall injure, deface or destroy any notices, rules or regulations for the government of the Park, posted or in any other manner permanently fixed by order or permission of the Commissioners of Fairmount Park within the limits of the same.

III. No person shall be permitted to bring led horses within the limits of Fairmount Park, or a horse that is not harnessed and attached to a vehicle, or mounted by an equestrian.

IV. No military or other parade or procession, or funeral shall take place in or pass through the limits of the Park, without the license of the Park Commissioners.

V. No person shall engage in any play, at base ball, cricket, shinney, foot ball, croquet, or at any other games with ball and bat, nor shall any foot race or horse race be permitted within the limits of the Park, except on such grounds only as shall be specially designated for such purpose.

VI. No person shall be permitted to use the shores of the river Schuylkill within the boundaries of Fairmount Park as a landing place for boats, or keep thereat boats for hire, nor floating boat houses with pleasure boats for hire, except by special license or lease granted by the Commissioners, to be paid for as the Commissioners shall from time to time direct, and only at places designated by and under restrictions determined upon by said Commissioners.

VII. No regatta or boat race by boat clubs, whose houses are built upon any part of the Park grounds, shall take place within the boundaries of the Park without special permission granted by the Commissioners, or by their Committee on Superintendence and Police.

VIII. No velocipedes shall be permitted to be used in Fairmount Park, except upon places that may be specially assigned for their use by the Committee on Superintendence and Police.

IX. Belmont avenue within the Park limits shall be kept in order, and used as a highway for burden traffic, as well as general travel for

I. No persons shall turn cattle, goats, swine, horses or other animals loose into the Park. Cattle, goats, swine, horses, &c.

II. No persons shall carry fire-arms, or shoot birds in the Park, or within fifty yards thereof, or throw stones or other missiles therein. Fire-arms, throwing stones, &c.

III. No one shall cut, break, or in anywise injure or deface the trees, shrubs, plants, turf, or any of the buildings, fences, structures or statuary, or foul any fountains or springs within the Park. Defacing trees, buildings, &c., and fouling springs, &c.

IV. No person shall drive or ride therein at a rate exceeding seven miles an hour. Rate of speed.

the accommodation of the public, in such manner as shall from time to time be directed by the Commissioners of Fairmount Park. (Resolution of October 16th, 1869.)

X. The passage of funeral trains and of droves of cattle, hogs, sheep and other animals over Belmont avenue within the boundaries of Fairmount Park is prohibited.

XI. No cattle, horses, sheep or hogs, shall be driven over any bridge across the river Schuylkill within the Park between the hours of ten A. M. and ten P. M.; nor during other hours of the day in greater numbers than ten cattle or horses, or twenty sheep or hogs, at any one time, nor such droves nearer together than three hundred feet, each drove being in charge of a man; nor shall any bull be driven in any such drove along with cows; and it shall be the duty of the Park Guard to enforce this regulation of the Park, by causing the separation of the animals at least three hundred feet from the bridge; and any driver of such animals who shall violate this regulation, or resist the Park Guard in its enforcement, shall pay a fine not exceeding five dollars, to be recovered as provided by law in respect to other Park fines.

XII. No person shall annoy, strike, injure, maim or kill any animal kept by direction of the Commissioners, either running at large or confined in a close.

Driving off roads.

V. No one shall ride or drive therein, upon any other than upon the avenues and roads.

Vehicles used for hire.

VI. No coach or vehicle used for hire, shall stand upon any part of the Park for the purpose of hire, nor except in waiting for persons taken by it into the Park, unless in either case at points designated by the Commission.

Vehicles of burden.

VII. No wagon or vehicle of burden or traffic shall pass through the Park, except upon such road or avenue as shall be designated by the Park Commissioners for burden transportation.(*a*)

Street railroad cars.

VIII. No street railroad car(*b*) shall come within the lines of the Park without the license of the Park Commission.

Articles exposed for sale.

IX. No person shall expose any article for sale within the Park without the previous license of the Park Commission.

Ice.

X. No person shall take ice from the Schuylkill within the Park without the license of the said Commission first had, upon such terms as they may think proper.

Indecent language, &c.

XI. No threatening, abusive, insulting, or indecent language shall be allowed in the Park.

Gaming, obscenity, &c.

XII. No gaming shall be allowed therein, nor any obscene or indecent act therein.

Bathing.

XIII. No person shall go in to bathe within the Park.

(*a*) See ante, page 36, note (*a*), rule IX.
(*b*) See Act of March 16, 1870, post, page 51.

XIV. No person shall fish or disturb the water-fowl in the pool, or any pond, or birds in any part of the Park, nor discharge any fire-works therein, nor affix any bills or notices therein. *Fish, water-fowl, birds, fire-works and notices.*

XV. No person shall have any musical, theatrical, or other entertainment therein, without the license of the Park Commissioners. *Entertainments.*

XVI. No person shall enter or leave the Park except by such gates or avenues as may be for such purpose arranged. *Entrance and exit.*

XVII. No gathering or meeting of any kind, assembled through advertisement, shall be permitted in the Park without the previous permission of the Commission ; nor shall any gathering or meeting for political purposes in the Park be permitted under any circumstances. *Political and other meetings.*

XVIII. That no intoxicating liquors shall be allowed to be sold within said Park. *Intoxicating liquors.*

SECT. 22. Any person who shall violate any of said rules and regulations, and any others which shall be ordained by the said Park Commissioners, for the government of said Park, not inconsistent with this act, or the laws and constitutions of this State and United States— the power to ordain which rules and regulations is hereby expressly given to said Commissioners—shall be guilty of a misdemeanor, and shall pay such fine as may be prescribed by said Park Commissioners,(*a*) not to exceed five *Commissioners shall have power to ordain other rules.* *Penalty for violation of rules.*

(*a*) The fine prescribed by the Commissioners is five dollars.

dollars for each and every violation thereof, to be recovered before any alderman of said city, as debts of that amount are recoverable, which fines shall be paid into the city treasury: *Provided*, That if said Park Commissioners should license the taking of ice in said Park, or the entry of any street railroad car(*a*) therein, or articles for sale, or musical entertainments, it may be with such compensation as they may think proper, to be paid into the city treasury: *And provided*, That any person violating any of said rules and regulations shall be further liable to the full extent of any damage by him or her committed, in trespass or other action; and any tenant or licensed party who shall violate the said rules, or any of them, or consent to or permit the same to be violated on his or her or their premises, shall forfeit his or her or their lease or license, and shall be liable to be forthwith removed by a vote of the Park Commission; and every lease and license shall contain a clause making it cause of forfeiture thereof for the lessee or party licensed to violate or permit or suffer any violation of said rules and regulations or any of them. It shall be the duty of the police appointed to duty in the Park, without warrant, forthwith to arrest any offender against the preceding rules and regulations, whom they may detect in the commission of such offence, and to take the person or persons so arrested forthwith before a magistrate having competent jurisdiction.

SECT. 23. All rents, license charges and fees; all fines, proceeds of all sales, except of lands purchased,(*b*) and profits of whatsoever kind to be collected, received, or

(*a*) See Act of March 16, 1870, post, page 51.
(*b*) See Sec. 13, ante, page 33.

howsoever realized, shall be paid into the city treasury, into the city treasury for Park purposes. as a fund to be exclusively appropriated by Councils for Park purposes, under the direction of said Commission : *Provided*, That moneys or property given or bequeathed Proviso. to the Park Commissioners upon specified trusts(*a*) shall be received and receipted for by their Treasurer, and held and applied according to the trust specified.

SECT. 24. That the Councils of the City of Philadel- Councils may improve approaches to the Park. phia be and they are hereby authorized to widen and straighten any street laid upon the public plans of said city, as they may think requisite to improve the approaches to Fairmount Park.

SECT. 25. That nothing in this act contained shall This act not to affect proceedings pending in court. suspend or affect any proceeding pending in court under any existing law ; but the same shall be proceeded in as if this act had not been passed.

SECT. 26. The damages for ground and property taken Land damages to be ascertained, &c., in same manner as provided in act of 1867. for the purpose of this act shall be ascertained, adjusted and assessed in like manner as is prescribed by the act to which this is a supplement.(*b*)

SECT. 27. The said Park Commissioners shall employ, Park police. equip, and pay a Park force, adequate to maintain good order therein and in all houses thereupon ; which force Shall be subject to the orders of the Mayor in any emergency. shall be subject to the orders of the Mayor upon any emergency ; and so far as said force shall consist of others

(*a*) See Sec. 17, ante, page 34.
(*b*) See Act of March 26, 1867, Sec. 3, ante, page 21, and Act of April 14, 1868, Sec. 5, ante, page 29.

How appointed and controlled.

than the hands employed to labor in the Park, it shall be appointed and controlled as the other police of the city.

Park Solicitor.

SECT. 28. [There shall be an additional assistant appointed by the City Solicitor, whose duty it shall be, under the direction of the City Solicitor, to attend to the assessments of damages, and to such other business of a legal nature connected with the Park as said Commissioners may require.](a)

(a) Repealed by the 5th section of the Act of January 27, 1870, post, page 49.

Act of April 21, 1869. P. L. 1194.

A FURTHER SUPPLEMENT

To an act entitled "An act appropriating ground for public purposes in the City of Philadelphia," approved the twenty-sixth day of March, Anno Domini eighteen hundred and sixty-seven.

SECTION 1. *Be it enacted by the Senate and House of Representatives of the Commonwealth of Pennsylvania, in General Assembly met, and it is hereby enacted by the authority of the same,* That it shall be lawful for the Fairmount Park Commissioners, in the name of the City of Philadelphia, to prevent and restrain the damage or the destruction of any trees and shrubbery upon any premises within the bounds described for the Fairmount Park, by the supplement to the act creating said Park, approved the fourteenth day of April, eighteen hundred and sixty-eight, although the compensation to the owners may not have been assessed or paid.

Commissioners may prevent damages to trees, &c., although land damages have not been assessed.

SECT. 2. That the Fairmount Park Commissioners shall have power, on behalf of the City of Philadelphia, to adjust the boundaries(*a*) of said Park with any railroad or canal company whose track, tow-path or canal navigation lies within or is bordering upon said Park, and with any other owner bounding upon the Park, and to receive and make the proper conveyances or releases in adjusting said boundaries as now provided by law,(*b*) and if an increase of width be conceded to any company or companies, or individuals, or an exchange of property be made, it shall be

May adjust boundaries of Park with railroad and canal companies and others.

To receive and make proper conveyances, &c.

(*a*) See post, page 45, Sec. 5.

(*b*) See Act of April 14, 1868, Sec. 13, ante, page 33.

Rate of compensation for property released or exchanged.

at a rate of compensation not less than a just and proportionate share of the cost of the whole property paid at any time by the City of Philadelphia, with lawful interest thereon, which compensation shall be paid into the sinking fund of said city, for the extinguishment of the Park loan.

To be paid into sinking fund.

All moneys raised for purchase of grounds,&c., to be kept separately.

SECT. 3. That all moneys raised by the City of Philadelphia by loans for the purchase of grounds for the Fairmount Park, and the construction and laying out the same, shall be kept separately by the treasurer of the said city, and shall be appropriated and paid for no other purposes.(*a*)

Commissioners may take possession of property after sixty days' notice, although damages have not been assessed.

SECT. 4. It shall be lawful for the said Park Commission, after having given sixty days' notice of an intention so to do, to take actual possession of any lands or property included within the boundaries of the Park, although the compensation or damages for the said grounds or property may not have been assessed or paid ;(*b*) and the City of Philadelphia shall thereupon become liable for the payment of the compensation or damages which may be awarded for taking such grounds, as of the date when said grounds and property were actually taken into possession,

In that event award to bear interest.

and with interest from such date: *Provided*, That before any such notice be given as hereinabove provided, the said

Commissions shall first make application for appointment of jury.

Park Commissioners shall have made an application to the court for the appointment of a jury according to the provisions of law.(*c*)

(*a*) See Act of April 14, 1868, Sec. 11, ante, page 32.

(*b*) See ante, page 28, note (*a*). See also Act of April 14, 1868, Sec. 9, ante, page 31.

(*c*) See Act of March 23, 1867, Sec. 3, ante, page 21.

SECT. 5. If in laying out and adjusting the grades of the boundary avenues of Fairmount Park, the configuration of the ground shall make it advantageous to vary from the boundaries(a) as now authorized by law, said Park Commissioners are hereby authorized and empowered to negotiate and agree with any owner or owners of ground bounding upon the Park, and so required for the proper location and adjustment of said boundary avenues, as to the price and conveyance thereof; and to that end may take and receive additional ground, or make exchanges or releases as the case may require: *Provided*, That the area of the said Park shall not be increased thereby.

Commissioners may vary the boundaries of the Park in adjusting boundary avenues, and take additional ground.

Provided the area of the Park is not increased.

In case of inability from any cause to fix the price of any land, or to adjust the terms of any exchange of ground required for the purpose aforesaid, the same shall be determined by a jury appointed for the purpose, in the manner provided in the act to which this is a supplement.(b)

If Commissioners cannot agree with owners of land, Jury shall be appointed.

SECT. 6. That it shall and may be lawful for the City Councils to confer upon said Park Commission, and for the Commission to accept, the care and management from time to time of any other grounds now appropriated or hereafter to be appropriated for park purposes within the City of Philadelphia.

Councils may confer care of other grounds upon Commissioners.

SECT. 7. No Park Commissioner, and no Solicitor acting for said Commission, and no person exercising any office, or holding any appointment under such Commission shall

Commissioners, Solicitor and officers not to receive

(a) See ante, page 43, Sec. 2.
(b) See Act of March 26, 1867, Sec. 3, ante, page 21. Under authority conferred upon them by the above section, the Park Commissioners have varied the northwest boundary of the Park.

compensa-
tion from
parties hav-
ing claims.

receive, either directly or indirectly, any compensation for any service rendered to any party having any claim of any kind, whether for land damages, or in any other manner arising against said Commission, or the city, excepting only the proper salary or compensation, if any, attached to his office, and any offence against the provis-

Under pen-
alty of expul-
sion from
office.

ions of this section shall be deemed a misdemeanor, and punishable by expulsion from office.

1st section
of the Act of
14 April,
1868—defin-
ing bounda-
ries—
amended.

SECT. 8. The first section(a) of an act of Assembly, approved the fourteenth day of April, Anno Domini one thousand eight hundred and sixty-eight, entitled "A supplement to an act entitled 'An act appropriating ground for public purposes in the City of Philadelphia,'" approved the twenty-sixth day of March, Anno Domini one thousand eight hundred and sixty-seven, shall be amended so that the same in describing the boundaries of Fairmount Park shall read as follows: "Beginning at "a point in the northeasterly line of property owned and "occupied by the Reading Railroad Company, near the "City bridge over the river Schuylkill at the Falls, where "said northeasterly line would be intersected by the line "dividing the property of H. Duhring, from that of F. "Stoever and T. Johnson, if the same were extended; "from thence in a southwesterly direction upon said divi- "ding line and its prolongation to the middle of the Ford "road;" and from thence the said boundary line shall proceed as in said first section is described. And furthermore, it is hereby declared to be the true intent and

All grounds
pertaining to

meaning of the fifth section(b) of said act, that all the

(a) Ante, page 25.
(b) Ante, page 29.

grounds pertaining to Fairmount Park, and mentioned *Park de-clared to be* and described in any of the sections of said act of As- *subject to all powers con-* sembly, shall be subject to all the powers, control and au- *ferred upon the Commis-* thority which is by force of law conferred upon the Com- *sioners.* missioners of Fairmount Park.

SECT. 9. It is the true intent and meaning of the act *Park dam-ages not to* entitled " An act appropriating ground for public pur- *bear interest* poses in the City of Philadelphia," approved March *until pay-ment is made* twenty-sixth, one thousand eight hundred and sixty- *or warrant is issued.* seven,(*a*) and of the supplement thereto, passed April four-teenth, one thousand eight hundred and sixty-eight,(*b*) and of the provisions of this further supplement, that no interest shall be allowed on damages for ground taken up to the time of their payment, or the issue of any warrant for their payment by the City of Philadelphia, excepting *Exception.* only such cases as are provided in the fourth section of this act.(*c*)

(*a*) Ante, page 19.
(*b*) Ante, page 25.
(*c*) Ante, page 44. See also, as to interest on Park damages before the passage of this act, ante, page 32, note(*a*).

Act of January 25, 1873. P. L 95.

A FURTHER SUPPLEMENT

To an act entitled "An act appropriating ground for public purposes in the City of Philadelphia," approved the twenty-sixth day of March, Anno Domini eighteen hundred and sixty-seven.

SECTION 1. *Be it enacted by the Senate and House of Representatives of the Commonwealth of Pennsylvania in General Assembly met, and it is hereby enacted by the authority of the same,* That it shall be lawful for the Court of Quarter Sessions of Philadelphia county to confirm the partial or special reports of Park juries, and to order payment by the City of Philadelphia, of the damages awarded to one or more owners of land from time to time, although the jury shall not specify therein by whom the damages are to be paid without prejudice to the rights and power of the same or any other jury appointed by the court to subsequently make inquiry as to the advantages of opening said Park to properties adjoining, or in the vicinity of the same, and by a subsequent partial or special report to determine what amount, if any, of said damages shall be paid by the City of Philadelphia, and what amount, if any, shall be paid by the property owners benefited, as now provided by law.[a]

SECT. 2. That the word "within" in section thirteenth of the act of the fourteenth of April, Anno Domini one thousand eight hundred and sixty-eight, relating to Fair-

[a] See Act of April 14, 1868, Sec. 13, ante, page 47, and Act of June 13, 1873, post, page 54.
[b] Ante, page 55.

mount Park, next after the words "beyond or" be altered to "without." *to "without."*

SECT. 3. That should any vacancy happen in any jury *Vacancies in Park juries, how filled.* now appointed or hereafter to be appointed, by death or resignation, removal or otherwise, it shall be lawful for the court to fill such vacancy from time to time as it may happen without prejudice to the validity of the proceedings: *Provided,* That every claimant shall have the *Every claimant shall be fully heard by whole jury or quorum thereof.* opportunity of being fully heard by the whole jury or a quorum thereof after any such new appointment.(a)

SECT. 4. That the Board of Park Commissioners shall *Annual report of Commissioners.* make their annual report to the Councils of the City of Philadelphia during the month of January, and not to the Mayor of said city as now provided by law.(b)

SECT. 5. That the twenty-eighth section(c) of the act *Twenty-eighth section of the Act of April 14th, 1868, repealed.* entitled "A supplement to an act entitled 'An act appropriating ground for public purposes in the City of Philadelphia,' approved the twenty-sixth day of March, Anno Domini one thousand eight hundred and sixty-seven," approved the fourteenth day of April, Anno Domini eighteen hundred and sixty-eight, shall be and the same is hereby repealed; and there shall be appointed by the Commissioners of Fairmount Park, a Solicitor, *Commissioners to appoint Park Solicitor. Duties.* whose duty it shall be under their direction to attend to the assessment of damages, and to such other business of a legal nature connected with the Park as the said Com-

(a) See Act of March 26, 1867, Sec. 3, and notes, ante, pages 21 and 22.
(b) See Act of April 14, 1864, Sec. 14, ante, page 34.
(c) See ante, page 42.

4

Compensa-
tion.

missioners may require, he shall receive during the present year and hereafter, until otherwise ordered by Councils, the same compensation as is now provided for the Assistant Solicitor named in the said twenty-eighth section.

Act of March 16, 1870. P. L. 451.

AN ACT

To secure to the citizens of the Commonwealth the free use and enjoyment of Fairmount Park in the City of Philadelphia, and to prevent the construction of any railroad therein.

WHEREAS, The City of Philadelphia under authority Preamble. conferred by an act of Assembly approved March twenty-sixth, Anno Domini one thousand eight hundred and sixty-seven, and the several supplements thereto, has purchased a large body of land within the limits of said city, and laid out and improved the same as a public Park known as Fairmount Park, and has expended several millions of dollars in the purchase and improvement of the same:

SECTION 1. *Be it enacted by the Senate and House of Representatives of the Commonwealth of Pennsylvania in General Assembly met, and it is hereby enacted by the authority of the same,* That the City of Philadelphia is hereby required to City required to maintain and keep open Fairmount Park. maintain and keep open the said Fairmount Park for the free use and enjoyment of all the citizens of this State, subject to the rules adopted for the good order and government of the same,(*a*) and in consideration of the compliance of the said city with the requirements of this In consideration whereof no railroads shall ever be built in the Park. Act, the State of Pennsylvania hereby declares and agrees that no railroad shall ever hereafter be constructed within the limits of the said Fairmount Park:(*b*) *Pro-*

(*a*) See ante, page 35, Sec. 21.
(*b*) See Act of Apr.l 14, 1868, Sections 19 and 20, ante, page 35.

Rights al-
ready ac-
quired by
railroad
companies
preserved.

vided, That nothing in this act shall be construed to interfere with the rights already acquired by any railroad company whose tracks are now laid within the limits of said Fairmount Park.

Act of March 15, 1871. P. L. 363

A FURTHER SUPPLEMENT

To an act appropriating ground for public purposes in the City of
Philadelphia, approved the twenty-sixth day of March, Anno
Domini, one thousand eight hundred and sixty-seven.

SECTION 1. *Be it enacted by the Senate and House of
Representatives of the Commonwealth of Pennsylvania in
General Assembly met, and it is hereby enacted by the authority of the same,* That the said Park Commissioners
shall have power to exclude from the Park manufactories
therein, so as to leave the ownership in the owners
thereof, with defined boundaries under agreements to be
made between the said owner and the City of Philadelphia, to run with the title, in manner to protect the
purity of the waters of the Schuylkill and the Wissahickon, and to preserve good order in the Park, and to
prevent the sale of intoxicating liquors upon any part of
the premises to be so left in private ownership; and such
exemption from being taken for public use, may be for a
term of years or in fee.

Commissioners may exclude from the Park manufactories therein. Under agreements with the owners. To protect purity of water. To preserve good order. To prevent sale of intoxicating liquors. Exemption may be for term of years or in fee.

SECT. 2. That it shall be lawful for the Fairmount
Park Commissioners to agree with the Ridge Avenue
Turnpike Company for the taking of said Ridge avenue,
from Dauphin street northwestward to the Wissahickon,
and if they cannot agree, to petition for a jury in manner
authorized by the acts relating to said Park; and such
jury shall proceed, and the court have all the power in
said acts contained, for the ascertainment and payment
of the damages for freeing said avenue from tolls.(a)

Commissioners may agree with Ridge Avenue Turnpike Company for portion of said turnpike. Upon failure to agree, jury may be appointed. Proceedings, &c.

(a) See Act of March 26, 1867, Sec. 3, ante, page 21.

Act of June 15, 1871. P. L. 391.

AN ACT

Relating to the assessment of damage for the appropriation of land
for public use.

SECTION 1. *Be it enacted by the Senate and House of
Representatives of the Commonwealth of Pennsylvania in
General Assembly met, and it is hereby enacted by the authority of the same,* That in all cases of the appropriation
of land for public use, other than for roads, streets or
highways, it shall not be lawful to assess, apportion or
charge the whole or any portion of the damage done to
or value of the land so appropriated, to, among or against
the other property adjoining or in the vicinity of the
land so appropriated, nor the owners thereof; and all acts,
or parts of acts, inconsistent herewith, are hereby repealed.(*a*)

No assessments for benefits shall be made upon property adjoining or in the vicinity of land taken for public use, except in the case of roads, &c.

(*a*) See Act of March 26, 1867, Sec. 3, ante, page 22. This act does
not apply to cases where part of the same tract of land is taken, and
part is not. In that case the jury is bound, in ascertaining the damages, to take into consideration the advantages to that portion of the
tract which is left: 20 Leg. Int. 220.

ORDINANCES.

*Ordinance of March 4, 1868, Ordinances 1868,
page 88.*

AN ORDINANCE

Appropriating ground for public purposes, pursuant to the Acts of
Assembly empowering the City of Philadelphia so to do ; also de-
fining the limits, and providing for the improvement of Fairmount
Park.

SECTION 1. *The Select and Common Councils of the City
of Philadelphia do ordain,* That Fairmount Park shall
consist of the area of water and of ground which is
embraced within the following limits, to wit, beginning
at a point in the northeasterly line of property owned
and occupied by the Reading Railroad Company, near
the city bridge over the river Schuylkill at the Falls,
where said northeasterly line is intersected by the line
dividing property of H. Duhring from that of F. Stoever
and T. Johnson, extending from thence in a southwesterly direction upon said dividing line and its pro.
longation to the middle of the Ford road ; from thence
by a line passing through the southeast corner of Forty-
ninth and Lebanon streets to George's Run ; thence along
the several courses of said run to a point fourteen hundred and eighty-seven and a half feet from the middle of
the Pennsylvania railroad, measured at right angles
thereto ; thence by a straight line through the northeast
corner of Forty-third and Hancock streets to the north-

Boundaries
of Fairmount
Park de-
fined.

erly side of Girard avenue near Fortieth street; thence
by the said northerly line of Girard avenue to the easterly side of the Junction railroad as now used; thence
by the said easterly side of the Junction railroad and
the Pennsylvania railroad to the north side of Haverford
street; thence by the northerly side of said Haverford
street to the westerly side of Bridgewater street; thence
by the said Bridgewater street to the north line of
Bridge street; thence by said Bridge street to the west
abutment of the Suspension Bridge; thence by the northwesterly side of the Suspension Bridge and Callowhill
street to the angle in said street, on the southwesterly
side of Fairmount Basin; thence by the northerly side of
Callowhill and Biddle streets to the westerly side of
Twenty-fifth street; thence by the said Twenty-fifth
street to the southwesterly side of Pennsylvania avenue;
thence by the said southwesterly side of Pennsylvania
avenue to the west side of Thirty-third street; thence
along the westerly line of Thirty-third street to the
southwesterly line of Ridge avenue; thence along said
Ridge avenue to the southwesterly line of South Laurel
Hill Cemetery (north of Huntingdon street); thence by
and along said property line to such a distance from the
shore line of the river Schuylkill as will permit the location of a carriage road one hundred feet wide upon its
margin; thence along the said river shore, and its several
courses, as may be most practicable, at the same distance
as above specified (provided said distance shall not exceed
one hundred and fifty feet), to a point opposite the intersection of the Ridge turnpike and School lane; thence
northwardly to a point on the southwesterly side of said
turnpike road, opposite to the southeasterly side of said

School lane; thence by the southwesterly side of the
Ridge turnpike road and its several courses to the southeasterly side of the Wissahickon creek; thence by the
several courses of the southeasterly side of Wissahickon
creek to the Schuylkill river; thence across the water
course of said river to the northeasterly line of the Reading Railroad Company's property, as now occupied and
in use, at the city boundary line; thence along said
northeasterly line, as now occupied and used by said
railroad company, to the place of beginning. Excepting,
nevertheless, hereout the several water works and their Water
appurtenances, which are included within these bounda- works ex-
ries, and such uses of the premises immediately adjacent
to the same, and such other portions of the ground as are
described in this section, as the city may from time to
time require for the purposes of its Water Department ;(a)
and saving the rights and franchises of the Schuylkill And also
Navigation Company, and the Philadelphia and Reading, certain cor-
Connecting and Junction Railroad Companies, as now porations.
provided by law.(b)

SECT. 2. That there shall be laid out and constructed a Roberts'
road of easy and practicable grades, extending from the drive pro-
intersection of the northerly line of the Park by Belmont vided for.
avenue, on the westerly side of the river Schuylkill, to the
head of Roberts' Hollow; and thence along the said hollow and the river Schuylkill to the foot of City avenue;
laid out with ground contiguous thereto for ornamentation, of such width and so constructed as the Commissioners of Fairmount Park, appointed under authority of

(a) See Act of April 14, 1868, Sec. 1, ante, page 25, wherein the
same boundaries are defined by act of Assembly.
(b) The franchises of the above corporations are also excepted by
the Act of April 14, 1868, Sec. 3, ante, page 28.

the act of the General Assembly of the Commonwealth, may determine. And the City of Philadelphia hereby declares its design and intent to make such road and its contiguous ground a part of the aforesaid Park ; and it hereby authorizes said Commissioners to ascertain by proper survey, and report its boundaries, so that the same

Commissioners shall lay out boundary avenues. may be duly appropriated.(*a*) And the said Commissioners shall in like manner lay out and cause to be opened an avenue outside of and extending along so much of the boundary of the Park as is between the point of beginning in the description given in the first section of this Ordinance and Girard avenue ; which new avenue shall be not less than one hundred feet in width ; and in like manner on the easterly side of the river they shall lay out and cause to be opened a similar avenue, extending outside of and along the Park boundary, from the intersection of Thirty-third street and Pennsylvania avenue ; northwardly and westwardly to the river

Commissioners authorized to exercise authority over boundary avenues, and so much of Girard avenue as lies within the Park. Schuylkill. And the said Commission are hereby authorized and empowered to exercise over the said new avenues, and also over so much of Girard avenue(*b*) as is included within the limits of the Park, such authority as may be requisite for their proper laying out, decoration, and improvement, and for their preservation as public highways adjacent to the Park.(*c*)

(*a*) See Act of April 14, 1868, Sec. 2, ante, page 27, wherein the Roberts' Hollow drive is provided for by act of Assembly.

(*b*) As a general proposition, but by no means universal, bridges are treated as portions of the highways which cross them, and are to be maintained by the same persons to whom the duty of repairing the highways is committed : 18 P. F. Smith, 406.

(*c*) So much of the above section as relates to the laying out and control of boundary avenues, has been modified by Sections 7 and 8 of the Act of April 14, 1868, ante, page 30.

SECT. 3. The City of Philadelphia hereby declares its intention to appropriate the shores of the Wissahickon creek, on both sides of the same, from its mouth to such point as may hereafter be determined, by said Park Commissioners, and of such width as may embrace the road now passing along the same, and may also protect the purity of the water of said creek, and preserve the beauty of the scenery upon its banks, so that the same may be hereafter added to Fairmount Park, and constitute a part of the same. And the said Commissioners of Fairmount Park are hereby authorized and empowered, with the aid of a proper survey, to define the appropriate limits of the ground proper to be taken for Park uses upon both shores of the Wissahickon, and to report the same for such definite legislation thereon as may be requisite and proper for the Councils of the City of Philadelphia.(a)

Declaration of intention to appropriate shores of Wissahickon creek.

Commissioners empowered to define the appropriate limits of ground to be taken, and report to Councils.

SECT. 4. The City of Philadelphia in pursuance of the several acts of Assembly enabling it so to do, and of any and all acts of the General Assembly of the Commonwealth conferring such power upon it,(b) does hereby appropriate and set apart forever the area of land and water comprised within the limits prescribed in the preceding sections of this ordinance, as an open public ground and Park for the preservation of the purity of the Schuylkill water, and of the health and enjoyment of the people forever.(c)

Area of land and water described in preceding sections set apart forever as a public park.

(a) The appropriation of the shores of the Wissahickon creek, and the manner of defining the Park boundaries thereon, is provided for by the 2d Section of the Act of April 14, 1868, ante, page 28.

(b) See post, page 63.

(c) See Act of April 14, 1868, ante, page 25.

Commissioners authorized to take possession of ground described in preceding sections, and to exercise control over and improve the same.

SECT. 5. That in addition to the powers conferred, by the act of Assembly creating the Commission, upon the Commissioners of Fairmount Park, the City of Philadelphia hereby authorizes and empowers said Commission to take possession of so much of the ground contained within the limits set forth in the preceding sections of this ordinance as may be beyond the limits of the ground appropriated by or under the act of Assembly establishing said Commission, and to exercise over the same, as part of Fairmount Park, all the powers and authorities which are requisite for its appropriation, its laying out

Subject to such appropriations as Councils may make.

and adornment, as part of the Park ;(a) subject, nevertheless, to such appropriation as may, from time to time, be made for such purposes by the Councils of the city.(b)

Commissioners authorized to negotiate with owners of land.

SECT. 6. That the said Commission be and they are hereby authorized and empowered to negotiate with the owners of so much of the land included within the aforesaid limits as is beyond the boundaries mentioned in the act of Assembly establishing the Commission(c) and to agree with them if it be practicable as to the price of their land,(d) and if it is not practicable so to do, that

Upon failure to agree, Law Depart-

the Law Department of the city be and the same is hereby authorized and directed, upon the request of said

---

(a) See Act of March 26, 1867, Sec. 1, ante, page 19, and Act of April 14, 1868, Sec. 3, ante, page 28, and Sec. 5, ante, page 29, and Act of April 21, 1869, Sec. 8, ante, page 46.

(b) So much of the above section as relates to appropriations, is modified by the 4th and 5th Sections of the Act of March 26, 1867, ante, pages 22 and 23, and by the 11th Section of the Act of April 14, 1868, ante, page 32.

(c) Act of March 26, 1867, ante, page 19.

(d) The same power is conferred upon the Commissioners by the Act of April 14, 1868, Sec. 26, ante, page 41.

Commission, to take proper steps in the law for the ascertaining and adjusting of the damages attending the taking of such land.(a)

(a) The clause relating to the Law Department is superseded by 3d Section of Act of March 26, 1867, ante, page 21, and 5th Section of Act of January 27, 1870, ante, page 49.

Resolution of January 24, 1871. Ordinances 1871, page 8.

RESOLUTION

Of request to the Commissioners of Fairmount Park and to the Legislature.

Resolved by the Select and Common Councils of the City of Philadelphia, That the Commissioners of Fairmount Park be requested to construct within the Park suitable fire-proof buildings for a public art gallery and museum for free exhibition at all times.

HUNTING PARK

AND

LEGACY OF ELLIOTT CRESSON.

Act of February 2, 1854. P. L. 43.

A FURTHER SUPPLEMENT

To an act, entitled "An act to incorporate the City of Philadelphia."

SECTION 39.   *   *   *   *   *   *   *

That it shall be the duty of the City Councils to obtain by dedication or purchase, within the limits of the said city, an adequate number of squares or other areas of ground, convenient of access to all its inhabitants, and lay out and maintain such squares and areas of ground as open public places, for the health and enjoyment of the people forever.

Councils required to obtain, and lay out public squares and parks.

Ordinance of July 10, 1856. Ordinances 1856,
page 177.

AN ORDINANCE

Relating to "Hunting Park," in the Twenty-third Ward, of the City
of Philadelphia.

Boundaries
of Hunting
Park de-
fined.

SECTION 1. *The Select and Common Councils of the City
of Philadelphia, do ordain,* That all that certain tract,
piece or parcel of ground, situate in the Twenty-third
Ward of the City of Philadelphia, commencing at a point
in the easterly line of the Old York road, now called
York avenue, and the middle of Nicetown lane (formerly
thirty-three feet wide, and now increased to the width of
sixty feet, by the addition of thirteen feet six inches on each
side, as agreed upon by the owners of property on each
side thereof); thence along the middle of said Nicetown
lane south, sixty degrees east, eighty-three perches and
forty-seven hundredths of a perch to a point; thence by
land of ———— ————, north, thirty degrees east,
thirty one perches and seven-tenths of a perch to a corner;
thence by land of ———— ————, north, twenty-seven
degrees five minutes west, eighty-six perches and two-
tenths of a perch to a corner; thence by land of the said
Jacob Steinmetz, north, one and one-half degrees east,
twenty-six perches and eight-tenths of a perch to a corner;
thence by the same west forty-five perches and eight-
tenths of a perch to the easterly line of the York avenue
aforesaid; thence along said easterly line of said York
avenue south, two degrees twenty-five minutes west,

eighty-nine perches and twenty-nine hundredths of a perch more or less to the place of beginning; containing about forty-three acres twenty-one and two-tenths square perches of land, the which premises were generously given to the City of Philadelphia by several of her citizens, as a free gift, to be used as a public park, free of access for all the inhabitants of the city, and for the health and enjoyment of the people, forever, be and the same is hereby devoted and dedicated to public use as and for a Park, and the said area of ground shall be called "Hunting Park."

SECT. 2. It shall not be lawful for any person or persons to sell or dispose of intoxicating liquors, or of merchandise of any kind whatsoever, within the boundaries of said Park; and if any person shall offend against the provisions of this ordinance, he or she so offending shall forfeit and pay for each offence the sum of twenty dollars, which penalty shall be sued for before any alderman of the City of Philadelphia, and the same being recovered, the informer shall be entitled to the one-half part thereof.

Sale of intoxicating liquors and merchandise prohibited.

Penalty for so doing.

How recovered.

SECT. 3. It shall be the duty of the Commissioner of City Property to cause the said Park to be laid out by some suitable and competent person, who shall be approved by the joint special Committee of Councils having charge of this subject, and upon such plan as the said Committee may, in conjunction with the Committee of the donors, consent to and approve; the said Committee shall report to Councils such plan and cost of same. And he shall also, subject to the like supervision and approval, cause the same to be planted with suitable and appropriate trees, and otherwise prepared for its future uses.

Commissioner of City Property required to cause said Park to be laid out, under certain restrictions.

5

Appropri-
ation there-
for.

SECT. 4. That the sum of four thousand dollars be and the same is hereby appropriated to meet the expenses which may be incurred in the execution of this ordinance, the same to be in lieu of any previous appropriation to this purpose.

Act of May 15, 1871. P. L. 873.

AN ACT

Enlarging the duties and powers of the Commissioners of Fairmount Park, by requiring them to take charge of Hunting Park in the City of Philadelphia, and of the legacy of Elliott Cresson, providing for the planting of trees in said city.

SECTION 1. *Be it enacted by the Senate and House of Representatives of the Commonwealth of Pennsylvania in General Assembly met, and it is hereby enacted by the authority of the same,* That the care and management of Hunting Park, in the City of Philadelphia, is hereby transferred and committed to the Commissioners of Fairmount Park, who shall be and they are hereby authorized and required to take charge of the same, and lay out, enclose, plant, and adorn the same; and who shall possess and exercise the like powers and authorities, in every particular, over the said Hunting Park, as now by existing laws, or hereafter by such as may be passed, they now have, or may hereafter come to have, over Fairmount Park, in the City of Philadelphia.

Care of Hunting Park transferred to Commissioners of Fairmount Park.

To lay out, enclose, plant and adorn the same. And to exercise like powers over the same as they exercise over Fairmount Park.

SECT. 2. It shall and may be lawful for said Commissioners to survey, locate, lay out and established an avenue,(a) which shall not be less than one hundred feet in width, which shall extend from Hunting Park to Fairmount Park, connecting the two Parks with each other, at such points as the Commissioners aforesaid may think best; and all and singular the provisions of exist-

Commissioners may lay out an avenue from Hunting Park to Fairmount Park. Land required there-for shall be

(a) See Act of April 4, 1872, Sec. 1, post, page 70.

acquired under laws pertaining to the acquisition of land for Fairmount Park. ing laws relating to Fairmount Park, concerning the mode of acquiring possession of land, and of the title to land, are hereby extended to the land and property necessary, in the judgment of said commission, to be required in order to the laying out and establishment of said avenue; the said avenue shall be laid out, paved and adorned as a Park road by said Commissioners, and shall be under their police control and supervision.

Said avenue shall be a Park road, and shall be under the control of the Commissioners.

Commissioners may make exchanges of land for the purpose of squaring said Park before Jan. 1st, 1872. SECT. 3. That for the purpose of squaring the said Hunting Park, and making the same more suitable in shape for use as a park, the Park Commissioners may negotiate with the owner of ground on the east side of said Hunting Park, and south side of Bristol street, and acquire the title to an area of ground, at least as large as all that part of the said Hunting Park situate north of the line of said Bristol street, which latter ground shall be given in exchange for the ground so acquired east of the said Hunting Park and south of said Bristol street, and a deed or deeds so agreed to be given in even exchange to the person entitled to receive the same, shall be executed by the Mayor of the City of Philadelphia whenever he shall be requested so to do by the Park Commissioners; and the said exchange to be made on or before the first day of January, one thousand eight hundred and seventy-two.(a)

Councils shall provide such moneys as the Commissioners may require. SECT. 4. It shall be the duty of the Councils of the City of Philadelphia from time to time, on the request of said Commissioners to provide such moneys as the said

(a) See Sec. 2, of the Act of April 4, 1872, post, page 71.

Commission may require for the proper execution of the duties imposed upon them by this act.

SECT. 5. The care and management of the legacy(a) made to the City of Philadelphia by the late Elliott Cresson of the sum of five thousand dollars, the income of which is to be applied to the planting of shade trees in said city, in accordance with the provisions of his will, is hereby assigned, appointed, and transferred to the Commissioners of Fairmount Park, who are hereby authorized and directed to receive, execute and discharge the said trust, and to whom the City of Philadelphia is hereby authorized to pay over any accumulation of interest and income now existing, and such as from time to time accrues for that purpose.

Care of the Elliott Cresson legacy transferred to the Park Commissioners.

(a) Extract from the will of Elliott Cresson, deceased. "Item.—I give and bequeath to the Mayor and Councils of Philadelphia the sum of $5,000 in trust, as a perpetual fund, the income from which I desire shall be annually forever expended in planting and renewing shade trees, especially in situations now exposing my fellow-citizens to the heat of the sun—desiring that due care be taken to select the best varieties of fine trees, and excluding such foreign trash, as the Lombardy Poplar, Ailanthus, Paper Mulberry and similar exotics." This is a good charitable bequest : 6 C. 437.

Act of April 4, 1872. P. L. 900.

A SUPPLEMENT

To an act, entitled "An act enlarging the duties and powers of the Commissioners of Fairmount Park, by requiring them to take charge of Hunting Park, in the City of Philadelphia and of the legacy of Elliott Cresson, providing for the planting of trees in said city."

Preamble.

WHEREAS, By the second section of the act to which this is a supplement, it is enacted that it shall and may be lawful for said Commissioners to survey, locate, lay out and establish an avenue which shall not be less than one hundred feet in width, which shall extend from Hunting Park to Fairmount Park, et cetera; now therefore,

Park Commissioners may open Bristol street instead of the avenue authorized by the 2d section of the act of May 15th, 1871, see ante page 67.

SECTION 1. *Be it enacted by the Senate and House of Representatives of the Commonwealth of Pennsylvania in General Assembly met, and it is hereby enacted by the authority of the same,* That the said Commissioners of Fairmount Park be authorized in their discretion, and they are hereby authorized to open, within a reasonable time, the street known as, or designated, Bristol street, on the plan of the City of Philadelphia, from Hunting Park to Fairmount Park, in the place and stead of the avenue authorized by the said second section(*a*) of the said act to be located,

Land required for said street, how acquired.

laid out and established; and that all and singular, the provisions of existing laws relating to Fairmount Park, concerning the mode of acquiring possession of land, and

(*a*) See Act of May 15, 1871, Sec. 2, ante, page 67.

of the title to land, are hereby extended to the land and property necessary, in the judgment of said Commissioners, to be required in order to the opening of said street; the said street may be opened, macadamized, adorned and kept in repair as a Park road by said Commissioners, and shall be under their police control and supervision. Shall be kept as a Park road.

SECT. 2. That in order to square the said Hunting Park, and to make the same suitable and more attractive in shape for the purposes of a Park, the said Commissioners may, in their discretion, negotiate with the owner of ground on the east side of Hunting Park and the south side of Bristol street, and may acquire the title to an area of ground as large as all that part of the said Hunting Park situate north of the line of the said Bristol street; which latter ground may be given in exchange for the ground so acquired east of the said Hunting Park and south of the said Bristol street, and a deed or deeds so agreed to be given in exchange to the person entitled to receive the same, shall be executed by the Mayor of the City of Philadelphia, whenever he shall be requested so to do by the Park Commissioners, and the said exchange to be made on or before the first day of July, one thousand eight hundred and seventy-three.(a) Commissioners may make exchanges of land to square Hunting Park before July 1st, 1873.

(a) See Act of May 15, 1871, Sec. 3, ante, page 63.

www.ingramcontent.com/pod-product-compliance
Lightning Source LLC
Chambersburg PA
CBHW021531270326
41930CB00008B/1203